4.98

WILLIAM SHAKESPEARE

THE HISTORIES

Richard III · King John · Richard II · Henry V

by

L. C. KNIGHTS

. . . the truth of what we are
shows us but this.   *Richard II*

PUBLISHED FOR
THE BRITISH COUNCIL
BY LONGMAN GROUP LTD

LONGMAN GROUP LTD
Longman House, Burnt Mill, Harlow, Essex

*Associated companies, branches and
representatives throughout the world*

First published 1962
Reprinted with additions to Bibliography 1965, 1971
© L. C. Knights, 1962, 1971

*Printed in Great Britain by
F. Mildner & Sons, London, EC1R 5EJ*

SBN 0 582 01151 5

CONTENTS

ILLUSTRATIONS

I. David Garrick (1717-79) as Richard III. Reproduced from the painting by William Hogarth at the Walker Art Gallery, Liverpool.

II. Alec Guinness as Richard II, in the Old Vic production of 1947.

III. Robert Helpmann as the dying King John in the Stratford-upon-Avon Memorial Theatre production of 1948.

IV. Design for production of *Henry V* by Charles Keane (1811-68) by Thomas Grieves and L. Lloyds. Reproduced from the water-colour at the Victoria and Albert Museum.

(between pages 30 and 31)

¶WILLIAM SHAKESPEARE was born at Stratford-upon-Avon and was christened in the Parish Church on 26 April 1564. He died at Stratford on 23 April 1616, and at some date before 1623 a commemorative monument was erected in his place of burial, the chancel of the Parish Church.

SHAKESPEARE:
THE HISTORIES

I

THE BACKGROUND

SHAKESPEARE wrote ten plays on subjects taken from English history, and although only four of them will be dealt with in this essay some general observations on 'the Histories' may be allowed to introduce the discussion of *Richard III*, *King John*, *Richard II* and *Henry V*.

To start with, although we shall all go on using the term 'Shakespeare's Histories', it would be as well if we could free ourselves from some misleading notions that go with it. 'The Histories' are better thought of not simply as History Plays—the dramatization of past events—but as political plays. The Histories or Political Plays, moreover, do not form an entirely distinct and homogeneous species of Shakespearean drama: as with 'Shakespearean Tragedy' the blanket-term covers very great variety, and we need to be aware of this as well as of important common elements; there is continuity, development, but there is no mere repetition, no common formula for each member of the series. Finally, even though a rough grouping of plays on 'historical' themes clearly has its uses, these plays are properly understood only when they are seen in relation to others that are not historical or, in any obvious sense, political.

The political plays have of course a more obvious reference to events and accepted ideas outside themselves than is the case, for example, with *Othello*, and this raises the question of the kind of equipment necessary for the student. Here again there are a few simple distinctions to be made. To understand, to enjoy and to profit from these plays what we most need is of course an interest in men and affairs, a lively feeling for literature, and a capacity for responding to each play as a work of art. Given that basic and indispensable equipment however (and without it book-loads of information are of little use), some kinds of knowledge extraneous to the plays can help to sharpen our vision. Shakespeare was not, as was once believed, almost entirely ignorant of formal history, keeping by him, as was suggested in the eighteenth century, a 'chuckle-pated Historian' to give him facts which he afterwards vamped up.[1] He read for himself in Hall and Holinshed, and his reading did more than give him events that could be represented on the stage; it prompted his thinking about actions and reactions in the public world. As readers of the Histories therefore we need to know something of the Tudor view of history; even more, perhaps, we need to know something of the main assumptions behind men's thinking about politics in the sixteenth century, of the clash of ideas about such subjects as law, power, government, and the relations of men in society. It remains to add that when we have equipped ourselves with some information of this kind we shall be very careful not to assume that Shakespeare, in any play, is simply reflecting 'Tudor ideas', or that he is accepting them uncritically as premises for a dramatic action—not, at all events, unless we have good warrant from the play itself. In almost all his plays Shakespeare combined in a remarkable way a sense of tradition—the ability to assimilate and learn from the past— and the freshness and independence of one who sees and thinks for himself; even when he seems to put most emphasis on traditional and received ideas he has a way of subjecting those ideas to the keenest scrutiny: which of course is how tradition is kept alive, and part of the debt we owe to genius.

The major themes and assumptions of English historical writing in the sixteenth century have been admirably described by E. M. W. Tillyard in the second chapter of his

[1] E. K. Chambers, *A Short Life of Shakespeare* (1933), pp. 242-3.

Shakespeare's History Plays—a book indispensable to the student. In the historians' treatment of the comparatively recent past the great theme was of course the slow and painful working out of the consequences of the deposition of Richard II and the providential accession of Henry Tudor by which the civil strife of more than half a century was brought to an end: 'So that all men'—in Hall's often quoted words—'(more clearer than the sun) may apparently perceive, that as by discord great things decay and fall to ruin, so the same by concord be revived and erected.' Nowadays we may feel a little ironic about the Tudor view of history, so convenient for the Tudor monarchs, just as we find it hard to stomach the use of Homilies appointed to be read in churches for absolutist propaganda. Perhaps fully to enter into the Tudor dread of renewed internal dissension it would be necessary to have some first-hand experience of the miseries of civil war—of how 'one doth rend the other of those that one wall and one foss shuts in' (*Purgatorio*, vi, 83–4). But a very little historical imagination should be enough to check our irony. When in 1548 Hall asked, 'what noble man liveth at this day or what gentleman of any ancient stock . . . whose lineage hath not been infested and plagued with this unnatural division?' it was no mere rhetorical flourish. For sixteenth-century Englishmen it must have been virtually self-evident that 'the union of the two noble and illustre families of Lancaster and York' was an act of Providence.

But the events that loomed largest in the eyes of English historians of the sixteenth century—the miseries of the Wars of the Roses—were only the most striking examples of processes at work in all times and all places. History, for all its immediate appeal to the human interest in story, in character and action, was essentially the record of a moral process: it taught lessons that could be applied to the understanding of the present and the conduct of affairs. As Louis B. Wright says, in his great work on the reading habits of the Elizabethans: 'The faith in the didactic value of history was not confined . . . to any social group in Tudor and Stuart England, because the belief was almost universal that a knowledge of the past furnished a valuable guide to the present.'[1] And when history was transposed into semi-fictional forms it was still the moral issue that was predominant. It was, in the words of one of the most popular compilations of the mid-sixteenth century, 'a mirror'. Thomas Baldwin, in his dedication of the first edition of *A Mirror for Magistrates* (1559) to 'the nobility and all other in office', declaring that God dealt sternly with corrupt governors, wrote:

How he hath dealt with some of our countrymen your ancestors, for sundry vices not yet left, this book . . . can show: which therefore I humbly offer unto your honours, beseeching you to accept it favourably. For here as in a looking glass, you shall see (if any vice be in you) how the like hath been punished in other heretofore, whereby admonished, I trust it will be a good occasion to move you to the sooner amendment.[2]

We need not concern ourselves just now with the rather sweeping assumption behind this (Baldwin himself admits that 'some have for their virtue been envied and murdered'); the important fact is that those who bought the *Mirror* in its successive editions—and its popularity continued until well into the seventeenth century—expected something more than information or entertainment; they expected moral examples drawn from the field of public life and great affairs.

Similar expectations and interests were also satisfied in the theatre. It is a matter of common knowledge that the

[1] *Middle-Class Culture in Elizabethan England*, chap. ix, 'The Utility of History', p. 301.

[2] *A Mirror for Magistrates*, ed. Lily B. Campbell, pp. 65-6. The motto on the title page of the early editions is, '*Felix quem faciunt aliena pericula cautum*'. On the conception of history as a mirror see Miss Campbell's Introduction, pp. 48-55. Compare *Gorboduc* (acted 1562), I.i. Chorus:

And this great king, that doth divide his land,
And change the course of his descending crown. . . .
A mirror shall become to princes all,
To learn to shun the cause of such a fall.

last ten or fifteen years of the reign of Queen Elizabeth I saw the performance of a very large number of plays on subjects drawn from English history. Some of these can properly be covered by the familiar description of 'chronicle play'—'a history transformed into a play' (Schelling); but a considerable number, including the most distinguished, are related more closely to the old political and social moralities —like, say, Skelton's *Magnyfycence* (1529-32), Sir David Lindsay's *Ane Satyre of the thrie estaitis* (c. 1540-52), or the anonymous *Respublica* (1553)—than they are to the straight 'chronicles': to use the convenient term coined by A. P. Rossiter, they were Moral Histories—'chronicle patterned on an abstract design'. In the Preface to his edition of the anonymous *Woodstock* (c.1591-4) Rossiter wrote:

'Moral History' is a form to be critically recognized, not as a primitive survival, with flat Abstractions masking as characters; but as a useful name for history-plays where the shadow-show of a greater drama of state plays continually behind the human characters, sometimes (as in Shakespeare) upon something as large as the cyclorama of the stars . . . However historical an Elizabethan play is, it is very little 'period': the writer's mind, like the stage itself (with its Elizabethan dresses and weapons), largely operated in a timeless sphere. Within that sphere, history was often presented as the conflict of principles.[1]

'Moral History'—in the sense in which *Woodstock* is a Moral History—is a category into which none of Shakespeare's plays fits with any ease, at all events, after the Henry VI sequence. (Rossiter himself makes this plain in his later book, *Angel with Horns*.) All the same, to recognize the existence of this *kind* of play is to bring about an important shift of focus when we try to see Shakespeare's Histories for what they are: for they too use historical material as a means of exploring fundamental principles of man's life in a political society.

[1] *Woodstock: a Moral History*, Preface, pp. 9-10 and *passim*. *Woodstock* itself 'is no "Chronicle-history-play"'. The chronicle materials are lifted from their time-sequence to operate in a timeless conflict of moral forces, in a strictly patterned plot' (p. 25).

Little can be said by one who is not a specialist in these matters about the political principles most likely to have influenced the mind of the young Shakespeare. Perhaps the best known principle of state concerned the necessity for authority, order and degree. There was as yet no fully developed theory of the divine right of kings, but it was natural that supporters of the Tudor monarchy should put a good deal of weight on the virtue of obedience in the subject. Not only was firm order in the state the only alternative to anarchy (in the later part of the century contemporary France seemed to reinforce the lesson of the Wars of the Roses), society was seen as part of the cosmic order with its parallel and corresponding 'planes of being', so that disorder at one level was echoed in the others. In the First Book of Homilies (1547), *An Exhortation Concerning Good Order and Obedience to Rulers and Magistrates* speaks of order in the heavens, on the earth, in man's body and mind, and in the state, and proceeds:

So that in all things is to be lauded and praised the goodly order of God: without the which no house, no city, no commonwealth can continue and endure; for, where there is no right order, there reigneth all abuse, carnal liberty, enormity, sin and Babylonical confusion. Take away kings, princes, rulers, magistrates, judges, and such estates of God's order, no man shall ride or go by the highway unrobbed; no man shall sleep in his own house or bed unkilled; no man shall keep his wife, children, and possessions in quietness; all things shall be in common; and there must needs follow all mischief and utter destruction both of souls, bodies, goods and commonwealths.[1]

This is the note that, after the failure of the Rebellion of the North, is formidably developed in the *Homily against Disobedience and Wilful Rebellion* (1570). Since the miseries of mankind sprang from Adam's disobedience, 'it is evident that obedience is the principal virtue of all virtues, and indeed the very root of all virtues, and the cause of all

[1] *The Two Books of Homilies Appointed to be Read in Churches*, ed. John Griffiths (1859), pp. 104-5.

felicity'. Rebellion, on the other hand, is 'worse than the worst government of the worst prince':

How horrible a sin against God and man rebellion is, cannot possibly be expressed according to the greatness thereof. For he that nameth rebellion nameth not a singular or one only sin, as is theft, robbery, murder and such like; but he nameth the whole puddle and sink of all sins against God and man; against his prince, his country, his countrymen, his parents, his children, his kinsfolk, his friends, and against all men universally; all sins, I say, against God and all men heaped together nameth he that nameth rebellion.[1]

This aspect of Tudor theory has been admirably described in recent works of scholarship, and in a general way is now sufficiently well known to students of Elizabethan literature.[2] But it is also important to remember that at no time did absolutist propaganda have an entirely free field. Besides positive law, there was Natural law (so powerfully expounded by Hooker); besides the idea of royal supremacy there was the idea of the moral responsibility of the ruler —the idea, even of the ruler as the 'representative' of the commonwealth: 'kings and princes ... are but members ... without a commonwealth there can be no king.' This last quotation is from John Ponet's *A Shorte Treatise of Politicke Power* (1556) which, according to Ponet's modern editor, was one of the signs, in mid-century, of a partial return to medieval conceptions of the limits of a prince's power: 'Even with the rise of strong national monarchy, the old restrictions did not entirely disappear from the English consciousness.'[3] How far these different currents of thought —derived from contemporary need and practice and from medieval tradition, from the Bible, Aristotle and Aquinas, and from many other sources—conflicted with and modified

---

[1] op. cit., p. 568.

[2] See the books by Tillyard, Spencer and Hart listed in the bibliography.

[3] Winthrop S. Hudson, *John Ponet* (1516?-1556), *Advocate of Limited Monarchy*. See also J. W. Allen, *A History of Political Thought in the Sixteenth Century*, Part II, chap. iii, 'The Very and True Commonweal'.

each other is something not easily determined. For the literary student there are perhaps two points in especial to be emphasized. The first is the simple fact that 'Tudor thought' on social and political matters was not entirely homogeneous: there was at all events sufficient diversity—indeed contradiction—to incite thoughtful men to thinking. The second is that a loyal and intelligent subject of Elizabeth I was likely to be conscious of other political matters besides what was due to the Prince. At the beginning of his masterly and lucid survey, *Political Thought in England: Tyndale to Hooker*, Mr Christopher Morris remarks of sixteenth-century Englishmen:

Most of all they discussed the importance to Society of obedience to authority, although they remained aware of limits which, in a healthy society, no authority would think of over-stepping. The King, more-over, was only one of the authorities. There were others—the Law, the People, the Church, God, and (according to some thinkers) Conscience. None of these authorities had as yet been conflated or confused with any other; and the problem facing social theorists was that of rendering to each authority its due.

In the early 1590s the author of *Woodstock* knew what response he would get from his audience when he made the bad Judge, Tresilian, say, 'It shall be law, what I shall say is law . . . I rule the law'.[1]

Where, then, did Shakespeare take his start? To that question only a study of the plays can provide an adequate answer. It can safely be asserted however that he was well aware of the 'educated' view of English history since the deposition of Richard II, and of the prevailing doctrine of the need for strong rule, order and degree, and of the heinousness of rebellion: aware of them, but not uncritical

---

[1] cf. Morris, op. cit., p. 83: 'Without doubt there was general agreement among Elizabethans that the king was not absolute in any but a highly technical sense, that he was not above the law, that law was not what he willed, that in so far as he ever made law, he made it in and through his parliament.'

of them; for each view, right up to a point, oversimplified.
The belief in historical nemesis, with its corollary of some
kind of mundane happy ending once guilt had been expiated,
left no room for a fact of history as fully attested as the
coming home of sins to roost.

> Just or unjust alike seem miserable,
> For oft alike both come to evil end.

For neither Shakespeare nor Milton was that a final answer:
all the same it represents a different order of thinking from
the easy moralizing of *A Mirror for Magistrates*, and it was a
thought not unlikely to have occurred to the author of
King Lear. As for the necessity for order, so often expounded
in this period, I know it is sometimes claimed that Shakespeare was a convinced exponent of what we should nowadays call the right-wing assumptions of his time; and there
are indeed passages in his work that testify to a horror of
anarchy. But order—especially order dependent on absolute
rule and unargued acceptance of the powers that be—was
not for Shakespeare a simple and unquestioned value:
essential order, simultaneously political and more-than-
political, was something that needed his full mature powers
to define and assert. What he gained from the historical
writing and the political assumptions of his time, though
not from these alone, was a conviction that politics and
morals cannot be separated without falsification and
disaster. That conviction lasted him a lifetime. More
narrowly formulated doctrines of the kind touched on
above served him in organizing historical material in his
earliest work; but as his mind played on them the current
simplifications were dissolved into something more subtle,
more far-reaching, more firmly related to the pressures of
experience. As A. P. Rossiter said: 'The Tudor myth
system of Order, Degree, etc., was too rigid, too black-and-
white, too doctrinaire and narrowly moral for Shakespeare's

mind: it falsified his fuller experience of men.'[1] The plays
now to be examined show Shakespeare developing a view
of history, of politics and public life, more searching than
anything to be found in his 'sources'.

II

RICHARD III

To call Shakespeare's Histories 'political' plays is simply one
way of indicating that they deal with such matters as the
nature of power—and the conflict of powers—within a
constituted society, and with the relation of political
exigencies to the personal life of those caught up in them.
In other words, they belong not with the limited class of
Elizabethan chronicle plays, but with that extensive range
of world literature that includes *Antigone*, *Athalie*, *The
Possessed* and *Under Western Eyes*. To say this is not of course
to offer a definition: it merely suggests the nature of the
interest that we bring to bear. What that interest finds to
engage and direct it in such plays as *Richard III* and *Julius
Caesar* is a matter for particular criticism: there is no
formula that will help us. But there is one preliminary
generalization that may be made. Shakespeare's early plays
show an increasingly subtle relation between observation
and what—for want of a better word—we may call inwardness. It is observation that strips off pretence, shows us how
the world goes, points a useful moral. But at its furthest
reach it can do no more than offer a truth that we acknow-
ledge about other people—the Bastard's 'Commodity, the
bias of the world', or Dr Stockman's summing up in *An
Enemy of the People*:

---

[1] *Angel with Horns, and Other Shakespeare Lectures*, 3, 'Ambivalence:
the Dialectic of the Histories', p. 59.

I only want to drum into the heads of these curs the fact that the liberals are the most insidious enemies of freedom—that party programmes strangle every young and vigorous truth—that considerations of expediency turn morality and justice upside down.

Inwardness on the other hand is not only the probing of character and motive, it involves the observer: some revelation of what is usually concealed prompts not only dramatic sympathy but a sense that something potential in the spectator is being touched on. It is the development of this quality that, above all, links the political plays with the great tragedies—with *Macbeth*, for example, which is simultaneously political play and universal tragedy. In the plays before us there is indeed no clear line of progression, but we shall, I think, appreciate more vividly what each play has to offer if we see it not simply as an isolated achievement but as pointing towards the masterpieces that lie outside the scope of this study.

Richard III (1592–3) is clearly linked to the three parts of *Henry VI* by what Dr Tillyard calls 'the steady political theme: the theme of order and chaos, of proper political degree and civil war, of crime and punishment'; but, unlike its predecessors, it is very much more than a dramatic presentation of the Tudor view of history. It is not simply a play about the providential accession of the House of Tudor, it is, in the first place, an elaborately formal dramatization of power-seeking in a corrupt world, held together by what Rossiter calls a 'basic pattern of retributive justice'.[1]

The formal pattern of the play has often been described, and certainly it is a contrivance of great ingenuity. Basically (as Dover Wilson, following Moulton, points out), it is composed of a complicated system of nemeses: crime brings punishment, for, in the words of York in *3 Henry VI*,

[1] Whether directly, or mediately through the chronicles, Shakespeare was deeply indebted to More's life of Richard, which was 'an attack on the non-moral statecraft of the early Sixteenth Century'. R. W. Chambers, *Thomas More* (1935), p. 117.

'Measure for measure must be answered', or, in the words
of Buckingham in this play, 'Wrong hath but wrong, and
blame [*sc.* fault] the due of blame'. Clarence (who broke
his promise to Warwick and was one of those who killed
Edward, the Lancastrian Prince of Wales) goes to his death
in the Tower just as Hastings is released. Hastings, hearing
of the death of the Queen's kindred at Pomfret, exults in
his own security:

> Think you, but that I know our state secure,
> I would be so triumphant as I am?   (III.ii.81-2)

just before he is hustled to his death by Richard and
Buckingham. Buckingham, 'the deep revolving, witty
Buckingham', who plays his part as Richard's 'other self'
with something of his master's swagger, breaks with
Richard partly because of the proposed murder of the
Princes, partly because he can't get payment for his services:
when he too falls and is led to execution, he recalls the false
oath with which he sealed his reconciliation with the
Queen's party:

> That high All-seer, which I dallied with,
> Hath turn'd my feigned prayer on my head,
> And giv'n in earnest what I begg'd in jest.   (V.i.20-2)

As for the arch-contriver, there is the succession of eleven
ghosts before Bosworth to remind him—and us—what he
is now paying for. This kind of repetition in the action
gives an effect of irony both to the mutual pledges and to
the boastful self-assertion of the characters; whilst at the
same time the device of formal accusation of one character
by another keeps the crimes committed constantly in view
—each is, as it were, his brother's bad conscience. The effect
is to present almost all these people as interlocked in a
'destiny' made of 'avoided grace' (IV.iv.219).

The formal patterning of the action is of course paralleled
in the verbal structure: 'the patterned speech of the
dialogue . . . is fundamentally one with the ironic patterns

of the plot' (Rossiter). I do not know whether rhetorical devices are more numerous here than in any other of Shakespeare's plays; they are certainly more obtrusive. No purpose would be served by listing the various figures of speech—alliteration, repetition, antithesis, stichomythia, and more recondite Elizabethan 'figures'—it is enough if we notice the stiff formal texture of so much of the verse:

> *Anne.* Lo, in these windows that let forth thy life
>   [the wounds of the dead Henry VI]
> I pour the helpless balm of my poor eyes.
> O cursed be the hand that made these holes!
> Cursed be the heart that had the heart to do it!
> More direful hap betide that hated wretch,
> That makes us wretched by the death of thee,
> Than I can wish to adders, spiders, toads,
> Or any creeping venom'd thing that lives!   (I.ii.12-19)

> *Gloucester.* Fairer than tongue can name thee, let me have
> Some patient leisure to excuse myself.
> *Anne.* Fouler than heart can think thee, thou canst make
> No excuse current but to hang thyself.
> *Glou.* By such despair, I should accuse myself.
> *Anne.* And, by despairing, shouldst thou stand excused
> For doing worthy vengeance on thyself,
> That did unworthy slaughter upon others.   (I.ii.81-8)

> *Q. Elizabeth.* If you will live, lament: if die, be brief.
>   (II.ii.43)

> *Duchess of York.* Dead life, blind sight, poor mortal living
>   ghost,
> Woe's scene, world's shame, grave's due by life usurp'd,
> Brief abstract and record of tedious days,
> Rest thy unrest on England's lawful earth,
> Unlawfully made drunk with innocent blood! (IV.iv.26-30)

These are characteristic examples; and the internal patterning of the verse is emphasized by the formal stance of the characters, as when Richard and Anne engage in a 'keen encounter of our wits', or when Queen Margaret makes a late appearance (clean contrary to historical fact and probability—'Here in these confines slily have I lurk'd') solely that she may join with Queen Elizabeth and the Duchess of York in a prolonged antiphonal lament that serves, once more, to recall the crimes and miseries of the past that have made the wretched present. Together, the elements of rhetorical speech and carefully balanced action combine to produce a complicated echoing effect of revenge and mutual wrong.

Yet what we have to do with is not a self-enclosed world of evil. The characters, it is true, move in a dense atmosphere of hatred, suspicion, treachery and fear, but the standards against which we, the spectators, are expected to judge 'the grossness of this age',[1] are firmly presented. This is not only a matter of explicit religious reference, as when the Second Murderer of Clarence surprisingly quotes Scripture—

> How fain, like Pilate, would I wash my hands
> Of this most grievous murder—   (I.iv.272-3)

Shakespeare had already at command more varied means of awakening the moral imagination. When compared with the second part of Clarence's dream, which is explicitly about hell, the first part may at first seem almost extraneous to the matter in hand: in fact it is an effective symbolist transformation of the more explicit moral commentary:

> Methought I saw a thousand fearful wracks,
> A thousand men that fishes gnaw'd upon,
> Wedges of gold, great anchors, heaps of pearl,
> Inestimable stones, unvalu'd jewels,

---

[1] Buckingham, objecting to the Cardinal's reluctance to fetch the young Duke of York from sanctuary:

> You are too senseless-obstinate, my lord,
> Too ceremonious and traditional.
> Weigh it but with the grossness of this age,
> You break not sanctuary in seizing him.   (III.i.44-7)

> All scatter'd in the bottom of the sea,
> Some lay in dead men's skulls; and, in the holes
> Where eyes did once inhabit, there were crept,
> As 'twere in scorn of eyes, reflecting gems. . . . (I.iv.24-31)

This, we may say, is a Shakespearean condensation of the contrast that runs all through Tourneur's *The Revenger's Tragedy*. At the other extreme is the dialogue on conscience between the murderers of Clarence:

First Murderer. How dost thou feel thyself now?

Second Murderer. Faith, some certain dregs of conscience are yet within me.

First Murderer. Remember our reward, when the deed's done.

Second Murderer. 'Zounds! he dies! I had forgot the reward.

First Murderer. Where's thy conscience now?

Second Murderer. O, in the Duke of Gloucester's purse.

First Murderer. When he opens his purse to give us our reward, thy conscience flies out.

Second Murderer. 'Tis no matter, let it go: there's few or none will entertain it.

First Murderer. What if it come to thee again?

Second Murderer. I'll not meddle with it: it makes a man a coward: a man cannot steal, but it accuseth him; a man cannot swear, but it checks him; a man cannot lie with his neighbour's wife, but it detects him. 'Tis a blushing shamefast spirit, that mutinies a man's bosom; it fills a man full of obstacles; it made me once restore a purse of gold that by chance I found; it beggars any man that keeps it; it is turn'd out of towns and cities for a dangerous thing; and every man that means to live well endeavours to trust to himself and live without it.   (I.iv.120ff.)

Irrelevant from the point of view of 'plot', this—which has obvious parallels in the later plays—is clearly a low-life variation on the main theme. ('Conscience', says Richard, when he has just suffered his worst defeat at its hands, 'is but a word that cowards use.') Nor, if we remember the Seven Deadly Sins in *Piers Plowman*, shall we find anything incongruous in the humour. The serious comedy of this scene is one more reminder that behind *Richard III* is the tradition of the morality play.[1]

Now all this, although necessary, has done little to bring into focus what it is that makes the play worth watching or reading, what makes it indeed characteristically Shakespearean: that is, the felt presence of a creative energy centering in, but not confined to, the figure of Richard of Gloucester. It is something that takes possession of our imagination as soon as Richard declares himself in his opening soliloquy:

> . . . Grim-visag'd War hath smooth'd his wrinkled front;
> And now, instead of mounting barbed steeds,
> To fright the souls of fearful adversaries,
> He capers nimbly in a lady's chamber,
> To the lascivious pleasing of a lute.
> But I, that am not shap'd for sportive tricks,
> Nor made to court an amorous looking-glass;
> I, that am rudely stamp'd, and want love's majesty,
> To strut before a wanton ambling nymph;
> I, that am curtail'd of this fair proportion,
> Cheated of feature by dissembling Nature,
> Deform'd, unfinish'd, sent before my time
> Into this breathing world, scarce half made up,
> And that so lamely and unfashionable,
> That dogs bark at me as I halt by them;
> Why, I, in this weak piping time of peace,
> Have no delight to pass away the time,
> Unless to spy my shadow in the sun,
> And descant on mine own deformity.
> And therefore, since I cannot prove a lover,
> To entertain these fair well-spoken days,
> I am determined to prove a villain. . . .   (I.i.9–30)

There is a colloquial vividness here that reminds us of Mosca's self-revelation at the opening of the third act of

---

[1] cf. Dover Wilson's Introduction to his edition of the play, pp. xvi–xvii. There is of course more sardonic humour in the scene (III.vii) in which Gloucester is 'persuaded' to accept the crown.

Volpone, but the total effect is quite un-Jonsonian. The idiomatic gusto—the pleasure in speaking words that have the well-directed aim of caustic popular speech—points forward to the Bastard, and will be an element in the poetry of all the greater plays. And this blends unobtrusively with effects of rhetoric and artifice: consider, for example, how the alliteration insists on a slight meaningful pause after 'spy' and 'descant' in the lines,

> Unless to spy my shadow in the sun,
> And descant on mine own deformity.

What is not Jonsonian is the felt presence of a world behind the lines—a world of strutting gallants and affected ladies, with, by contrast, the dogs barking at the malformed Richard; and behind this, pressing on it, is the private world of the man who has always felt himself to be outside the world's game and will, in consequence, simply play his own.[1]

It is the energy with which Richard plays his part—forthright wooer, plain blunt man, reluctant king ('O! do not swear, my Lord of Buckingham'), satirical commentator on the world's affairs and Machiavellian schemer—it is this that makes him into a commanding figure. But we should certainly be wrong to regard him solely as an 'engaging monster' to whose successful contrivance we give a reluctant admiration. Not only is Richard, like the other political figures, placed firmly within a framework of explicit moral reference, the energy that informs his language also manifests itself in other ways. I do not intend to take up again the question of 'character' in Shakespeare.[2] It is clear that if Shakespeare was intent on something more than—something different from—the presentation of life-like characters,

[1] There is an excellent account of this soliloquy by D. A. Traversi in his essay, 'Shakespeare: the Young Dramatist', *The Pelican Guide to English Literature*, 2, *The Age of Shakespeare*, pp. 180-2.

[2] See my essay, 'The Question of Character in Shakespeare', in *More Talking of Shakespeare* (1959), edited by John Garrett.

his figures are never merely embodied abstractions: in some sense we feel them as if they were persons, and we are made explicitly aware of those aspects of their assumed life history (Othello's generalship, Coriolanus' ties to his mother) that are relevant to the main design. In the case of Richard of Gloucester this means that Shakespeare compels us to take into account, and to give full weight to, his deformity—and his rancour at his deformity—that is insisted in on his first soliloquy. When, in Act II, scene iv, young York retails the gossip, picked up from his mother, that his uncle Gloucester was born with teeth, it seems a mere repetition of the legend to which Gloucester had himself subscribed in *3 Henry VI* (V.vii.53–4 and 70ff.). The effect, however, is very different; for whereas in the earlier play the abnormality seemed little more than part of the stock legend of the monster ('which plainly signified That I should snarl and bite and play the dog'), the present context enforces a change of tone and implication. Gloucester—his mother has just told us—'was the wretched'st thing when he was young', and this unobtrusive substitution of the real for the conventional momentarily shifts the balance of our sympathies and antipathies, just as when, later, young York gives his uncle a 'scorn' about his hunchback (III.i.128–35). There is, to be sure, no attempt to blur judgement with a sentimental 'understanding'. But the fact remains that in the presentation of the zestfully sardonic villain there are some disturbing reverberations:

> A grievous burthen was thy birth to me;
> Tetchy and wayward was thy infancy;
> Thy school-days frightful, desperate, wild and furious. . . .
>   (IV.iv.168–70)

It does not seem fanciful to say that this—from a further exchange between mother and son—presents in miniature the Delinquent's Progress to a manhood that is 'proud, subtle, sly, and bloody' (IV.iv.172).[1]

[1] See Grace Stuart, *Narcissus: a Psychological Study of Self Love* (1956).

In *Richard III*, although the various conventions are not yet welded into a unity, the connexion between linguistic vitality and energy of moral insight is already apparent. It is not only that Richard's lively idiom 'cuts through the muffled hypocrisies of language'.[1] Even in the elaborately stylized scenes Shakespeare is aiming at something more subtle than a self-conscious display of rhetorical skill: these too can precipitate a moment of lucid truth about human nature; as when Anne gives a somnambulistic half-assent to Richard (' would I knew thy heart') when he has woven round her his net of sophistries, which she knows to be such (I.ii.33–224), or when Queen Elizabeth, engaged in a formal rhetorical duel with Richard (IV.iv.376–80), shows him, step by step, that there is nothing he can swear by and be believed—neither honour, nor self, nor religion:

> Q. *Eliz.* Swear then by something that thou hast not wrong'd.
> K. *Rich.* Then, by myself—
> Q. *Eliz.*   Thyself is self-misus'd.
> K. *Rich.* Now, by the world—
> Q. *Eliz.*   'Tis full of thy foul wrongs.
> K. *Rich.* My father's death—
> Q. *Eliz.*   Thy life hath it dishonour'd.
> K. *Rich.* Why then, by God—
> Q. *Eliz.*   God's wrong is most of all.

But perhaps the most striking example of artifice working in the service of psychological realism is the climactic scene of Richard's visitation before Bosworth by the ghosts of his victims (V.iii.119ff.). Judged by the standards of the later Shakespeare the stiffly formal projection of suppressed guilt is crudely done. But this 'morality masque', this 'homily in fancy dress', does not stand alone; it leads directly to Richard's soliloquy on awakening:

[1] 'In scorn or indignation, such writers as Dickens, Heine and Baudelaire sought to cut through the muffled hypocrisies of language.' George Steiner, *Tolstoy or Dostoevsky* (1960), p. 25.

> O coward conscience, how dost thou afflict me!
> The lights burn blue. It is now dead midnight.
> Cold fearful drops stand on my trembling flesh.
> What do I fear? myself? there's none else by:
> Richard loves Richard; that is, I am I.
> Is there a murderer here? No. Yes, I am.
> Then fly. What, from myself? Great reason: why?
> Lest I revenge. What, myself upon myself?
> Alack, I love myself. Wherefore? for any good
> That I myself have done unto myself?
> O, no! alas, I rather hate myself
> For hateful deeds committed by myself. . . .   (V.iii.179–90)

Touches of melodrama should not prevent us from seeing
that Richard's dialogue with himself is, as Palmer says, 'no
empty catechism, but a dialogue pointed at the heart of the
eternal problem of conscience and personality'. It not only
points forward to the deeper searchings of the self-division
caused by evil in *Macbeth*, it helps to explain why *Richard
III* is so much more than an historical pageant, more even
than a political morality play. It is one instance among
others of Shakespeare's sure sense—his sane, sure probing—
of what lies behind the heavy entanglements of public
action.

III

KING JOHN

Shakespeare's *King John* (c.1594) has no relation to Bale's
King Johan (c.1539; revised 1560–3), which may be
mentioned here for two reasons. Bale's play is violent
Protestant propaganda, his King virtually a martyr to the
corrupt power of Rome:

> This noble King John, as a faithful Moses,
> Withstood proud Pharaoh, for his poor Israel,
> Minding to bring it out of the land of darkness. . . .

Some at least of Shakespeare's first audience must have been familiar with this tradition and have noticed what he did *not* say. Secondly, although John is supposed to stand for an historical person, the other characters are either allegorical ('England, a widow') or hover uneasily between allegory and history (Sedition is also Stephen Langton, and Private Wealth, Cardinal Pandulph): in other words the play takes its place in a category only recently recognized in which the old morality technique is used for contemporary religious or social purposes.

Shakespeare's direct source is the anonymous *The Troublesome Reign of King John*, published in two parts in 1591, in which the action makes some claim to being historical. *The Troublesome Reign*, although not so tedious as Bale's play, and although it provides a first sketch of the Bastard, is a sprawling affair. If Shakespeare's dramatic skill is evident in the form that he imposed on mere chronicle material it is because he shaped his original, and thereby transformed it, in the light of an idea—something of which *The Troublesome Reign* is innocent. It wasn't merely a matter of toning down the anti-Roman Catholic bias, or of excising the less promising scenes and reshaping the rest, or, even, of developing the Bastard into a vigorous 'character'. What Shakespeare set himself to do was to present international power politics in the realistic spirit in which he had presented the manœuvring for power within one country in *Richard III*.

The attempt, it must be admitted, is not entirely successful. Partly this is because the chronicle material was recalcitrant. More important, if we exclude Constance and Arthur (and the rhetoric of Constance's laments has little to do with true feeling), there is no point at which any kind of inward life is seen: the play is entirely governed by 'observation'. Within these marked limitations what we are given is of course often superb; and Faulconbridge, the main commentator on the action, represents the clear emergence in Shakespeare's work of an element that he was to transcend but never entirely to abandon. In spite of his royal blood the Bastard is, in the society in which he finds himself, an outsider—the shrewd young man up from the country; and his vigorous colloquial speech matches the keenness of his perception of all forms of humbug, whether social or diplomatic. The tone is set in the sprightly imaginary dialogue in which he sees himself engaging in the inanities of polite conversation in 'worshipful society' (I.i.189ff.). He is the solvent of all that is pretentious and unreal, whether it is the political rhetoric of the Citizens of Angiers ('He speaks plain cannon fire, and smoke and bounce'), or the love rhetoric of the Dauphin and some Elizabethan sonneteers, or diplomatic profession not matched by performance.

The world into which he is introduced is the world of 'policy', of Machiavellian statecraft. John is a usurper, whose 'strong possession' is much more than his 'right'. This however does not prevent him from publicly announcing himself as 'God's wrathful agent'. On the other side King Philip of France, joining the Duke of Austria in 'a just and charitable war', makes much of the religious sanctions of his support of Arthur, of his 'hospitable zeal' in the young Prince's cause, and so on. None of which prevents him from patching up a peace with England by means of a politic marriage between John's niece and the Dauphin, in which the bride is to bring four provinces as her dowry. That the peace is immediately broken at the instigation of the papal Legate does not affect the force of the Bastard's pivotal speech on 'commodity', or self-interest, which closes the first section of the play:

> Mad world! mad kings! mad composition!
> John, to stop Arthur's title in the whole,
> Hath willingly departed with a part:
> And France, whose armour conscience buckled on,
> Whom zeal and charity brought to the field
> As God's own soldier, rounded in the ear
> With that same purpose-changer, that sly devil,
> That broker, that still breaks the pate of faith,
> That daily break-vow, he that wins of all,

> Of kings, of beggars, old men, young men, maids,
> Who, having no external thing to lose
> But the word 'maid', cheats the poor maid of that,
> That smooth-faced gentleman, tickling Commodity. . . .
> And this same bias, this Commodity,
> This bawd, this broker, this all-changing word,
> Clapp'd on the outward eye of fickle France,
> Hath drawn him from his own determined aid,
> From a resolved and honourable war,
> To a most base and vile-concluded peace. . . .   (II.i.561-79)

This looks forward to the remainder of the action as well as back. There is indeed none of the anti-Catholic bias of the earlier John plays, but Pandulph is a wordly prelate, playing the world's game: having broken the league between the French and English kings he coolly expounds to the Dauphin how the news of his invasion of England is likely to cause John to put Arthur to death, thus strengthening the Dauphin's claim to the English throne. On John's politic submission he thinks to dismiss the French forces that he has used for his own purposes:

> It was my breath that blew this tempest up,
> Upon your stubborn usage of the Pope;
> But since you are a gentle convertite,
> My tongue shall hush again this storm of war. . . .
>
> (V.i.17-20)

The 'gentle convertite' meanwhile has become a murderer —in intention if not in effect—whose bad conscience is reflected in political ineptitude and an inglorious end. The Dauphin, on the other hand, has attempted to double-cross the English lords who, deserting from a bad king to a foreign invader, are caught in the contradictions of political action:

> . . . such is the infection of the time,
> That, for the health and physic of our right,
> We cannot deal but with the very hand
> Of stern injustice and confused wrong.   (V.ii.20-3)

The weakness of the play is seen in the conclusion. The revolted English lords, learning of the Dauphin's treachery, return to their allegiance. Salisbury has a lofty speech about this:

> We will untread the steps of damnéd flight,
> And like a bated and retired flood,
> Leaving our rankness and irregular course,
> Stoop low within those bounds we have o'erlooked,
> And calmly run on in obedience,
> Even to our ocean, to our great King John. . . .
>   (V.iv.52–7)

The last line, severely qualified though it is by the context of the play, does not seem to be intended ironically: it is simply preparing the way for the patriotic finale which can be contrived when John is dead and a new king proclaimed who does not share his guilt:

> This England never did, nor never shall,
> Lie at the proud foot of a conqueror,
> But when it first did help to wound itself . . .
>   . . . nought shall make us rue,
> If England to itself do rest but true.   (V.vii.112ff.)

This passage is certainly an improvement on the corresponding lines in *The Troublesome Reign*, and there is no reason to doubt Shakespeare's patriotism. But it is difficult to see here, as some have done, an explicit statement of the main theme of the play. In none of Shakespeare's plays does the ending simply cancel out—though it may modify—anything that has been strongly built into the body of the action, and on most of what has been unfolded before us our comment can only be the Bastard's 'Smacks it not something of the policy?' It is 'policy' and its entanglements that are engaging Shakespeare's interest. And although this may be seen with an almost cynical amusement, as in the Commodity speech, there are hints of a deeper awareness of what is involved in the clash of rival interests, as in the

sombre poetry of the Bastard's comment as Hubert carries
away the body of the dead Arthur:

> I am amazed, methinks, and lose my way
> Among the thorns and dangers of this world.
> How easy dost thou take all England up!
> From forth this morsel of dead royalty,
> The life, the right and truth of all this realm
> Is fled to heaven: and England now is left
> To tug and scamble and to part by th' teeth
> The unowed interest of proud-swelling state. . . .
> Now happy he whose cloak and cincture can
> Hold out this tempest. (IV.iii.140-9)

Observation of the public world, when as keen-edged as the
Bastard's, ends in perplexity and misgiving, and by itself
can go no further. In order to explore the nature of the
'tempest' caused when right and truth are fled, leaving only
appetite and interest, naked or disguised, Shakespeare
needed to relate more firmly his portrayed public action to
the inner lives of men.[1]

IV

RICHARD II

Richard II (1595) is a political play with a difference. Draw-
ing on events known to everyone as leading to the English
civil wars of the fifteenth century, it presents a political
fable of permanent interest: for what it shows is how
power—hardly conscious of its own intentions until the
event fulfils them—most necessarily fill a vacuum caused
by the withdrawal of power.[2] But behind the public frame-

---

[1] See John F. Danby, *Shakespeare's Doctrine of Nature*, pp. 68-9.

[2] See Brents Stirling, *Unity in Shakespearian Tragedy*, chap. iii. As so
often with Shakespeare's Histories, Marvell's 'An Horatian Ode' provides
a useful gloss:

> Nature that hateth emptiness,
> Allows of penetration less. . . .

work attention is concentrated on *the kind of man* who plays the central role. Richard is more than an unkingly king, he is an egotist who, like egotists in humbler spheres, constructs an unreal world that finally collapses about him. And it is because the political interest cannot be separated from the psychological interest—is indeed dependent on it—that *Richard II* is a different kind of play from *King John:* in some important ways it looks back to *Richard III* and forward to *Julius Caesar* and *Macbeth.*

That Richard is a king, and not simply a man, and that the play is about the deposition of a king—these are cardinal dramatic facts; and most of Richard's actions have to do with the exercise of kingly power, or the failure to exercise it. What we should think of the King the play leaves in no doubt. Of the king-becoming graces named in *Macbeth* (IV.iii.91ff.) Justice stands first, and Richard is not just. The matter of Gloucester's death though referred to with some explicitness (I.ii), lies outside the action of the play, but the whole of the first two acts portrays an arbitrariness and self-will that respects neither persons nor established rights. Richard is an extortionate landlord of his realm; he is brutal and unjust towards Gaunt; and in depriving Boling-broke of his inheritance he strikes at the foundations of his own power:

> Take Hereford's rights away, and take from time
> His charters and his customary rights;
> Let not tomorrow then unsue to-day;
> Be not thyself; for how art thou a king
> But by fair sequence and successionʔ   (II.ii.195-9)

Action is reinforced by explicit commentary. Richard's behaviour is a 'rash fierce blaze of riot' (II.i.33); it is 'vanity' (II.i.38); it is a 'surfeit' that will inevitably bring its 'sick hour' (II.ii.84). At the turning point of the action the gardeners are introduced for no other purpose than to moralize the event:

II. Alec Guinness as Richard II, in the Old Vic production of 1947

III. Robert Helpmann as the dying King John in the
Stratford-on-Avon Memorial Theatre production, 1948

IV. Design for production of *Henry V* by Charles Keane (1811-1868) by Thomas Grieves and L. Lloyds

> *First Servant:* Why should we, in the compass of a pale,
> Keep law and form and due proportion,
> Showing, as in a model, our firm estate,
> When our sea-walled garden, the whole land,
> Is full of weeds? . . .
>   *Gardener.*   Hold thy peace—
> He that hath suffered this disordered spring
> Hath now himself met with the fall of leaf . . .
>   . . . and Bolingbroke
> Hath seiz'd the wasteful king. O, what pity is it
> That he had not so trimm'd and dress'd this land
> As we this garden! . . .
>   Superfluous branches
> We lop away, that bearing boughs may live;
> Had he done so, himself had borne the crown,
> Which waste of idle hours hath quite thrown down.[1]
>
>   (III.iv.40ff.)

If however 'the political moral of *Richard II* is clear . . . it is not simple' (Brents Stirling). Richard's misdeeds do not justify his deposition—and this not because Shakespeare has passively accepted the doctrine of the sanctity of kingship and the sinfulness of rebellion. Gaunt, it is true, proclaims passive obedience before 'God's substitute, His deputy anointed in His sight', but this is balanced by the unavoidable questions prompted by Richard's own development of the theory of divine right (III.ii.36ff.). What guides us here is simply Shakespeare's appraisal of necessary consequences. It may be argued that Carlisle's impassioned prophecy before the deposition is prophecy only in appearance—Shakespeare had read Holinshed and knew what happened in the fifteenth century. But Shakespeare is not merely offering wisdom after the event; he is intent on causes and consequences, on the laws of human behaviour, as in Richard's rebuke to Northumberland after the deposition:

---

[1] It is a mistake to play this scene as a simple mixture of humour and pathos: the Gardener, who is not a stage rustic, has a genuine 'authority'. For the history of the comparison of the state to a garden see Peter Ure's Introduction to the New Arden edition, pp. li-lvii.

> thou shalt think,
> Though he divide the realm and give thee half,
> It is too little, helping him to all. . . .
> The love of wicked men converts to fear,
> That fear to hate. . . .   (V.i.6off.)

This is the way things happen in the game of power, and although Bolingbroke returns initially to claim what is justly his, he is no more—even if, confronting Richard's 'vanity', he is no less—than a man of power. In short, the play presupposes no possibility of a simple solution to the political situation: as Rossiter says, 'Richard is wrong, but Bolingbroke's coronation is not right; and Richard's murder converts it to the blackest wrong'. York's words apply to *both* sides—'To find out right with wrong—it may not be' (II.iii.145).

Within this clearly delineated framework of a political dilemma—this soberly realistic mapping of one of history's cunning passages—interest centres on the man who is Richard II. He is early shown as petulant and wilful; but what the play focuses with especial clarity is the fact that he is a self-deceiver, a man who imagines that a habitable world can be constructed from words alone. As with many figures in the later plays, essential attitudes are embodied in a manner of speech which simultaneously 'places' them. On Richard's return from Ireland some sixty lines are devoted to this purpose alone:

> I weep for joy
> To stand upon my kingdom once again.
> Dear earth, I do salute thee with my hand,
> Though rebels wound thee with their horses' hoofs.
> As a long-parted mother with her child
> Plays fondly with her tears and smiles in meeting,
> So weeping, smiling, greet I thee, my earth,
> And do thee favours with my royal hands;
> Feed not thy sovereign's foe, my gentle earth,
> Nor with thy sweets comfort his ravenous sense,
> But let thy spiders that suck up thy venom

> And heavy-gaited toads lie in their way,
> Doing annoyance to the treacherous feet,
> Which with usurping steps do trample thee;
> Yield stinging nettles to mine enemies. . . .   (III.ii.4-18)

—and so on. There follows Richard's elaborate comparison of the king to the sun, leading into an assertion of divine right:

> Not all the water in the rough rude sea
> Can wash the balm off from an anointed king:
> The breath of wordly men cannot depose
> The deputy elected by the Lord;
> For every man that Bolingbroke hath press'd
> To lift shrewd steel against our golden crown,
> God for his Richard hath in heavenly pay
> A glorious angel. . . .   (III.ii.54-61)

The sequence prompts various reflections. Most obviously Richard has not been a 'mother' to his land (we last saw him ordering the seizure of Bolingbroke's possessions, and we have been told of his other exactions): this bit of make-believe is almost as fantastic as the notion that Bolingbroke would be troubled by spiders. Richard of course does not expect to be taken seriously—'Mock not my senseless conjuration, lords', he says: the trouble is that it is impossible to draw a line between this fanciful self-dramatization and the more seriously intended assertion of royal power that follows. Not only does the repeated use of the first person singular ('my earth'!) undermine the royal 'we' when it appears (III.ii.49-50), Richard's assumption that heavenly powers will aid a king is seen, in this context, as not very different from the admittedly fanciful invocation of the English soil; indeed the religious references—as with the 'three Judases' later (III.ii.132)—only serve to underline the fearful discrepancy between Richard's self-deceiving rhetoric and reality. On a later speech in which self-dramatization is followed by foolish and irrelevant fantasy

(III.iii.143ff.) Dr Johnson commented, 'Shakespeare is very apt to deviate from the pathetic to the ridiculous'; but it is Richard, not Shakespeare, who thus deviates.

Shakespeare however is using the figure of Richard for a more serious purpose than the exhibition of a particular kind of kingly incompetence. *Richard II* is not universal tragedy, as *Macbeth* is; nevertheless what lifts it above the previous political plays is the way in which reality breaks into the closed world of the self-deceiver. The deposition scene (IV.i.162ff.) begins equivocally: there is dignity and pathos, but there is also the familiar self-regarding dramatization and habit of word-play. It is at the end of a passage of restrained rhetoric—beginning, characteristically, 'Now, mark me how I will undo myself'—that the process of recognition begins. There is indeed no sudden illumination, and the process is difficult to define without extensive quotation, but there is something that can properly be called a break-through from the depths of the nature that Shakespeare has imagined. It can be felt in the changed tone. Whereas Richard's earlier manner had been almost feminine, it is now masculine and direct. At the end of Richard's speech of self-deposition, the question, 'What more remains?' (IV.i.222) may be read as 'exhausted' (Traversi) or as an abrupt descent from rhetoric. What can be in no doubt is that from now on Richard sees himself without disguise:

> Must I do so? and must I ravel out
> My weaved-up follies? . . .
> Nay, if I turn mine eyes upon myself,
> I find myself a traitor with the rest. . . .
>   . . . I'll read enough
> When I do see the very book indeed
> Where all my sins are writ, and that's myself.   (IV.i.228ff.)

It is this new tone that underprops the pathos ('Mine eyes are full of tears, I cannot see'), and makes the subsequent play with the mirror something different from mere self-

indulgent theatricality: as Derek Traversi says, 'artificiality,
conscious self-exhibition, and true self-exploration are
typically blended':

> Was this the face
> That every day under his household roof
> Did keep ten thousand men? Was this the face
> That like the sun did make beholders wink?
> *Was this the face that faced* [trimmed] *so many follies* . . . ?
>
> (IV.i.281-5)

In more senses than one Richard is a man at bay, for he is
exposed to himself as well as to his enemies.[1] It is a bleak
awakening, as he admits with a sparse directness in the
moving scene of his parting from his wife (V.i):

> Learn, good soul,
> To think our former state a happy dream;
> From which awak'd, the truth of what we are
> Shows us but this.

Richard still *sees* his own story (V.i.40ff.); but he also sees
his own 'profane hours', and the verse in which he fore-
tells to Northumberland the consequences of usurpation
(V.i.55ff.) is unusually forthright.

The scene of the murder firmly establishes this new move-
ment. Richard's thought is still fanciful (something not unlikely in solitary confinement) and his expression 'conceited';
but the more fanciful passages end with a return to the
idiomatic and forthright:

> While I stand fooling here, his Jack o'the clock. . . .
>
> Spurr'd, gall'd, and tir'd by jauncing Bolingbroke;   (V.v.)

and there is no turning away from the painful reality.

---

[1] It is worth noticing how Shakespeare contrives to give the *feel* of
Richard's isolation, not only by what is said but by what is not said:
like Richard, we are aware of Bolingbroke's meaningful taciturnity
('Mark, silent king . . .') and of the eyes fixed on the central figure. The
climax ('Then give me leave to go.'—'Whither?'—'Whither you will,
so I were from your sights.') is masterly.

Richard recognizes his own sins:

> And here have I the daintiness of ear
> To check time broke in a disorder'd string;
> But for the concord of my state and time
> Had not an ear to hear my true time broke:
> I wasted time, and now doth time waste me.... (V.v.45-9)

And this in turn is accompanied by a recognition of the vanity of a life lived without some transforming principle that takes the self beyond the self:

> Nor I, nor any man that but man is,
> With nothing shall be pleas'd, till he be eas'd
> With being nothing.   (V.v.39-41)

The expected death comes abruptly—'How now! what means death in this rude assault?' Editors find this line perplexing, but the meaning is surely clear: death has not come in any of its fancifully imagined forms (III.ii.155ff.), it is simply brutal. In a sense the play ends with the heavily stressed monosyllabic line,

> thy fierce hand
> Hath with the king's blood stain'd the king's own land.
>   (V.v.109-10)

Those scenes of the last act from which Richard is absent, showing glimpses of the new world in which Bolingbroke rules, seem in some ways perfunctory and immature, and it is hard to take much interest in Aumerle's abortive conspiracy or the scene in which the Duchess of York pleads for her son's life. Sometimes the verse descends to doggerel, which may perhaps be, as Dover Wilson thinks, left over from an older play—though it is hard to see why Shakespeare should have let his attention lapse at just these points. It is indeed difficult to be sure of the reason for the unevenness of the last act, but certainly the poor verse of V.iii and V.vi makes the scene of the murder (V.v) stand out in strong contrast—and this not only in an easy theatrical effectiveness. Bolingbroke exercises kingly power with more firmness than Richard had done, and he shows clemency to Aumerle; but—and there is a parallel here with the opening scenes of the play—behind the public exercise of kingly rights lies illegality, and an act so bad that it can only be hinted at. It seems at least possible that the explanation of the silly rhymes and the almost farcical note of parts of the Aumerle scenes is that all this is intended to emphasize the superficial character of authority divorced from the moral foundations of rule. The reality is murder:

> Riddles lie here, or in a word—
> Here lies blood. . . .

As Traversi suggests, Bolingbroke's 'absorbing pursuit of power' is, in the nature of things, not likely to lay firmer foundations than Richard's abnegation of responsibility. The world of the unsuccessful egotist has collapsed; the nature of the world constructed by the realist politician, Henry IV, will be shown in the plays that bear his name.

V

HENRY V

Between *Richard II* and *Henry V* stands *Henry IV*, and neither of the two Parts of that play fits very happily into any generalizations we might be tempted to make about 'the Histories'. Indeed, as I have suggested elsewhere, the second Part is at least as closely related to the tragedies as it is to the historical sequence. All the same, *Henry IV* is in one of its aspects a political Morality of the kind that Dover Wilson describes in *The Fortunes of Falstaff*: Justice triumphs over Iniquity, and Hal, escaping from Feigning Flatterers, emerges as the type of the Prince, the Ruler. Now, in

Henry V (1599), Shakespeare—a popular playwright after all—finds himself committed to showing the Ruler in action. If the play does not entirely succeed it is partly because it is ostensibly devoted to a public theme in which we cannot quite believe; and the impression we get from the play is that Shakespeare did not believe in it either.

Certainly there is much in the play that can be cited by those who believe that Shakespeare's king is simply the hero of popular legend:

> Never came reformation in a flood,
> With such a heady currance, scouring faults. . . .   (I.i.33-4)

Canterbury and Ely describe him at length as the Renaissance complete man—able to reason in divinity and state affairs, eloquent, and yet a man of action. We may not entirely trust these worldly prelates, but it is a Chorus that speaks of him as 'the mirror of all Christian kings'; Henry emphatically declares that his 'passions' are subject to his 'grace' (I.ii.242); and he wishes to wage war with equity:

> ... we give express charge that in our marches through the country there be nothing compelled from the villages, nothing taken but paid for, none of the French upbraided or abused in disdainful language; for when lenity and cruelty play for a kingdom, the gentler gamester is the soonest winner.   (III.vi.105ff.)

He is aware of 'the fault my father made in compassing the crown', and he hopes by penitence to cleanse his rule of that stain. He is the embodiment of military heroism, the successful leader in war; he is 'free from vainness and self-glorious pride' (V. Chorus); and he shows himself capable of mixing easily with the common people. Nevertheless the play is something very different from a simple glorification of the warrior king. When we give full weight to all its parts—not simply to those in which Henry is favourably presented—we see that Shakespeare's attitude is complex and critical.

The patriotic theme is developed in the declamatory and unsubtle verse of the Choruses.[1] But what they give is only the public view of the public theme—'an abstract of average public opinion' (Goddard): there are also realistic 'close-ups' which bring in some deflationary irony. The second Chorus for example ('Now all the youth of England are on fire . . . and honour's thought Reigns solely in the breast of every man') is immediately followed by the first meeting of Bardolph, Nym and Pistol. Pistol 'shall sutler be Unto the camp, and profits will accrue'. As he says later (II.iii.52-4):

> Yoke-fellows in arms,
> Let us to France; like horse-leeches, my boys,
> To suck, to suck, the very blood to suck.

We should not of course make too much of the sociological significance of Pistol & Co.: they are obviously stage-comics, and Bates and Williams are the genuinely representative figures among the common soldiers. But Shakespeare knew that they were among the 'cull'd and choice-drawn cavaliers' eulogized in the third Chorus; he knew what the war meant to them; and he knew what was likely to happen to the disbanded riff-raff when the war was over (V.i.83-5):

> Old I do wax, and from my weary limbs
> Honour is cudgelled. Well, bawd I'll turn,
> And something lean to cut-purse of quick hand. . . .

A similar qualifying irony plays round some (not all) of the more famous passages of military exhortation. In Henry's long speech calling on the citizens of Harfleur to capitulate, Shakespeare's voice speaks through—and in a sense opposed to—the voice of the King, thus firmly 'placing' the sentiments expressed:

[1] 'The lines given to the Chorus have many admirers; but the truth is, that in them a little may be praised, and much must be forgiven.' Dr Johnson.

> The gates of mercy shall be all shut up,
> And the flesh'd soldier, rough and hard of heart,
> In liberty of bloody hand shall range
> With conscience wide as hell, mowing like grass
> Your fresh-fair virgins and your flowering infants. . . .
> What rein can hold licentious wickedness
> When down the hill he holds his fierce career?
> We may as bootless spend our vain command
> Upon the enraged soldiers in their spoil
> As send precepts to the leviathan
> To come ashore. . . .   (III.iii.10-20)

There is much more to the same effect. Now Henry is of course painting the bloodiest possible picture in order to win Harfleur without fighting: when the city gives in his order is, 'Use mercy to them all'. All the same, Shakespeare has been at pains to describe in detail some of the almost inevitable consequences of war. And this is not the only occasion on which he reminds the audience that there is more than one way of responding to a successful military campaign. We can for example put side by side the English and the French versions of the battle of Crécy:

> *Canterbury.*   . . . Edward, the Black Prince,
> Who on the French ground play'd a tragedy,
> Making defeat of the full power of France;
> Whiles his most mighty father on a hill
> Stood smiling to behold his lion's whelp
> Forage in blood of French nobility.   (I.ii.105-10)

> *French King.*   . . . Edward, Black Prince of Wales;
> Whiles that his mountain sire, on mountain standing,
> Up in the air, crown'd with the golden sun,
> Saw his heroical seed, and smil'd to see him,
> Mangle the work of nature, and deface
> The patterns that by God and by French fathers
> Had twenty years been made.   (II.iv.56-62)

We have here in little—in the clash between the admiring 'Forage in blood' and the regretful 'Mangle the work of

nature . . . '—an example of something that is not made
fully explicit until the play is near its end: it is the contrast
between a limited and inadequate ideal of manliness and
one that is fully adequate and mature. Henry's first speech
before Harfleur—'Once more unto the breach, dear friends'
(III.i)—does not represent the war poetry of the play at
its best. It is rhetorical in the bad sense, the imagery is forced
and unnatural, and it compares very unfavourably with the
King's address to his men before the battle of Agincourt
(IV.iii). All the same, it is not only the speech from the play
that every schoolboy knows, it represents an important part
of the attitude to life embodied in the figure of the hero-
king. How inadequate this is is fully revealed when, in the
last scene, Burgundy makes his great plea for peace
(V.ii.31-62):

> . . . let it not disgrace me
> If I demand before this royal view,
> What rub or what impediment there is,
> Why that the naked, poor, and mangled Peace,
> Dear nurse of arts, plenties, and joyful births,
> Should not in this best garden of the world,
> Our fertile France, put up her lovely visage?
> Alas! she hath from France too long been chas'd,
> And all her husbandry doth lie on heaps,
> Corrupting in it own fertility.
> Her vine, the merry cheerer of the heart,
> Unpruned dies; her hedges even-pleach'd,
> Like prisoners wildly overgrown with hair,
> Put forth disorder'd twigs; her fallow leas
> The darnel, hemlock and rank fumitory
> Doth root upon, while that the coulter rusts
> That should deracinate such savagery;
> The even mean, that erst brought sweetly forth
> The freckled cowslip, burnet, and green clover,
> Wanting the scythe, all uncorrected, rank,
> Conceives by idleness, and nothing teems
> But hateful docks, rough thistles, kecksies, burrs,
> Losing both beauty and utility.

> And as our vineyards, fallows, meads, and hedges,
> Defective in their natures, grow to wildness,
> Even so our houses and ourselves and children
> Have lost, or do not learn for want of time,
> The sciences that should become our country,
> But grow like savages, as soldiers will
> That nothing do but meditate on blood,
> To swearing and stern looks, defus'd attire,
> And every thing that seems unnatural. . . .

This beautiful passage—which in its ease and complexity reminds us that Shakespeare is now reaching the height of his powers—is not only free from the emotional straining that marks the Harfleur speech; it offers a positive ideal of civilization that is no mere abstraction but that brings with it the felt presence of the lived activities in which the ideal may be embodied. 'Behind the image of life and nature run wild for lack of human care is the implied ideal of natural force tended and integrated into a truly human civilization'[1] human, but still rooted in nature: in Milton's words, 'Growth, sense, reason, all summ'd up in man'.

Seen in this light it is hard to regard the play as a simple glorification of heroic leadership, even if, with Dover Wilson, we find that Henry's character is deepened and humanized after Harfleur. Rather I should agree with Traversi that the effect of the play as a whole is 'to bring out certain contradictions, human and moral, which seem to be inherent in the notion of a successful king'. Although Shakespeare presents with understanding the heightened fellowship of those sharing a common danger, and the responsiveness of the good general to the needs of the situation, there is only one scene where Henry gains a full measure of our sympathy—and that in spite of the fact, or because of the fact, that we do not entirely agree with him. I refer of course to the masterly scene near the opening of Act IV, where the King, disguised and under cover of darkness, talks with the common soldiers before the battle of

---

[1] L. C. Knights, *Some Shakespearean Themes*, p. 128.

Agincourt. There is no need to comment on the surface realism—admirably done—of the soldiers' comments:

> *Bates.* He [the King] may show what outward courage he will, but I believe, as cold as a night as 'tis, he could wish himself in Thames up to the neck, and so I would he were, and I by him, at all adventures, so we were quit here.   (IV.i.112ff.)

The ensuing conversation—so unforced in tone, and yet so telling in all its details—poses the dilemma of political leadership when force is accepted as a necessary instrument of policy: and it is a real dilemma, not one admitting of any simple solution. To the King's claim that his cause is just and his quarrel honourable Williams replies with a curt, 'That's more than we know'; and he goes on to insist on the grave moral responsibility of the ruler:

> But if the cause be not good, the king himself hath a heavy reckoning to make, when all those legs and arms and heads, chopped off in a battle, shall join together at the latter day, and cry all 'We died at such a place'; some swearing; some crying for a surgeon; some upon their wives left poor behind them; some upon the debts they owe; some upon their children rawly left. . . . Now, if these men do not die well, it will be a black matter for the king that led them to it; who to disobey were against all proportion of subjection.   (IV.i.133ff.)

Henry replies with a variety of arguments, too long to quote here, leading to the conclusion, 'Every subject's duty is the king's; but every soldier's soul is his own': *how* each soldier dies is his own concern. It is an interesting speech, in conscious intention sincere, and each statement in it taken singly is true or, at least, more than merely plausible. But it does not all add up to what Henry thinks it does. The analogies on which Henry relies so heavily are not perfect analogies: the master who sends his servant on a journey, in which the servant is set upon and killed 'in many irre-conciled iniquities', is not an exact equivalent for the king who leads his subjects to war. The King has brought his men to fight ('Then imitate the action of the tiger'), and, says Williams, 'I am afeard there are few die well that die in battle; for how can they charitably dispose of any thing when blood is their argument?' That contention could, I think, be answered, but Henry does not answer it. He simply shifts the responsibility. And the mood of the whole tragic argument finds its natural issue in the famous soliloquy:

> Upon the king! let us our lives, our souls,
> Our debts, our careful wives,
> Our children, and our sins lay on the king!
> We must bear all. O hard condition!
> Twin born with greatness. . . .   (IV.i.126–30.)

—ending with the nostalgic vision of a life free from the weight of responsibility which is all the king gets in return for his vain 'ceremony'.

The even division of sympathy in this scene—with the cutting edge of the argument, all the same, directed against Henry—suggests something of the complexity of attitude that informs the play as a whole. It is not resolved. As M. Fluchère says, 'While making the necessary concessions to patriotic feeling . . . Shakespeare lets us see . . . that the political problem, linked with the moral problem, is far from being solved by a victorious campaign.' In short, the political problem, conceived purely in terms of politics and the political man, is insoluble.

In *Julius Caesar*, written in the same year as *Henry V*, freed from the embarrassments of a patriotic theme, and with the problem projected into a 'Roman' setting, Shakespeare examined even more closely the contradictions and illusions involved in political action. But is *Julius Caesar* a History, a Political Play, or a Tragedy? In a sense the futility of the question provides an answer to it. When history is conceived in terms of a living present, it becomes a spur to the political intelligence; when the political intelligence is that of a Shakespeare—nourished, moreover, by a tradition in which political action is seen primarily as social, and ultimately as individual, action—then the action of that intelligence on its material will almost necessarily bring into view some of the profoundest questions of human nature. What gives Shakespeare's early political plays their distinctive quality is the fact that they are part of the same continuous, and continually deepening, exploration of the nature of man that includes the great tragedies. Why that should be so I have tried to indicate in the preceding pages, and by way of summary I should like to use the words of a critic whose understanding of Shakespeare was informed by a rare wisdom and humanity. Speaking of the material that Shakespeare made use of for the very first of his Histories, the late Professor Goddard wrote: 'Here, writ large, was the truth that chaos in the state is part and parcel of chaos in the minds and souls of individuals, that the political problem is, once and for all, a function of the psychological problem.' Later in the same study Professor Goddard says: 'Perhaps education will some day revert to a perception of what was so like an axiom to Shakespeare: that psychology goes deeper than politics and that a knowledge of man himself must precede any fruitful consideration of the institutions he has created.'

---

[1] Harold C. Goddard, *The Meaning of Shakespeare*, Chicago, 1951, Vol. I, pp. 29; 147.

SHAKESPEARE:
THE HISTORIES
Richard III · King John · Richard II · Henry V

A Select Bibliography

(Books published in London, unless stated otherwise)

Full bibliographical descriptions of the separate quarto editions and of the first collected edition of *Mr William Shakespeare's Comedies, Histories & Tragedies*, 1623 (the FIRST FOLIO) are given in W. W. Greg, *A Bibliography of the English printed drama to the Restoration*, 4 vols 1939–59.

ABBREVIATIONS

EC	*Essays in Criticism*
EETS	*Early English Text Society*
ELH	*Journal of English Literary History*
JEGP	*Journal of English and Germanic Philology*
MLQ	*Modern Language Quarterly*
MLR	*Modern Language Review*
PMLA	*Publications of the Modern Languages Association of America*
PQ	*Philological Quarterly*
REL	*Review of English Literature*
RES	*Review of English Studies*
SB	*Studies in Bibliography*
SEL	*Studies in English Literature 1500–1900 (Rice Univ.)*
ShJ	*Jahrbuch der deutschen Shakespeare-Gesellschaft*
ShQ	*Shakespeare Quarterly*
ShS	*Shakespeare Survey*
SP	*Studies in Philology*
ShSt	*Shakespeare Studies* (Cincinnati)
TSLL	*Texas Studies in Language and Literature*
UTQ	*University of Toronto Quarterly*

TEXTUAL STUDIES

CHAMBERS, E. K. *William Shakespeare: a study of facts and problems*; Oxford, 1930. I., pp. 294–305, 348–56, 364–7, 388–96.
WALKER, A. *Textual problems of the First Folio*; Cambridge, 1953.

GREG, W. W. *The editorial problem in Shakespeare*, 3rd ed; Oxford, 1954, pp. 68–70, 77–88, 120–1, 142–3.

—— *The Shakespeare First Folio*; Oxford, 1955, pp. 190–9, 236–9, 248–55, 282–8.

SISSON, C. J. *New readings in Shakespeare*, II, 1956.

CRAIG, H. *A new look at Shakespeare's Quartos*; Stanford, 1961.

CONTEMPORARY BACKGROUND SOURCES

BROOKE, C. F. T. ed. *The Shakespeare Apocrypha*; Oxford, 1908. (Edward III, Sir Thomas More.)

BULLOUGH, G. ed. *Narrative and dramatic sources of Shakespeare*, III (1960), pp. 221–349, 353–491; IV (1962), pp. 1–151, 347–432.

ELYOT, Sir T. *The Boke named the Governour*, 1531

—new ed. in Everyman series, 1962.

HALL, E. *The Union of the two noble and illustre famelies of Lancastre and York*, 1548

—ed. Sir H. Ellis, 1809.

GRIFFITHS, J. ed. *The two books of Homilies appointed to be read in churches*; Oxford, 1859

—'An Exhortation concerning good order and obedience', 1547; 'An Homilie agaynst disobedience and wylful rebellion', 1570.

HOLINSHED. *Chronicles of England, Scotland and Irelande*, 1577

—selection, ed. A. and J. Nicoll, Everyman, 1927.

HOOKER, R. *Of the lawes of ecclesiasticall politie*, 1594

—Book I and Introduction, Everyman, 1954.

LINDSAY, SIR D. *Ane Satyre of the thrie estaitis*; Edinburgh, 1602

—ed. J. Kinsley, 1954; also in 'Works', ed. D. Hamer, Scottish Text Society, 1931–6.

A Mirror for Magistrates, 1559

—ed. L. B. Campbell, Cambridge, 1938.

Respublica, 1553

—ed. W. W. Greg, *EETS*, 1952.

Woodstock: a moral history, 1591–4, ed. A. P. Rossiter, 1946; also in *Elizabethan history plays*, ed. W. A. Armstrong, 1965.

SACKVILLE, T. & NORTON, T. *Gorboduc*, 1565

—ed. A. K. McIlwraith, 'Five Elizabethan tragedies', World's Classics, 1938.

SKELTON, J. *Magnyfycence*, 1529–32.

—ed. R. L. Ramsay, *EETS*, 1908.

BACKGROUND: SECONDARY

COLERIDGE, S. T. 'On the principles of political knowledge'. [In *The Friend*, 1809]
—reprinted 1904, etc.

SCHELLING, F. E. *The English chronicle play*, 1902.

POLLARD, A. W. and others. *Shakespeare's hand in the play of Sir Thomas More*; Cambridge, 1923.

ALEXANDER, P. *Shakespeare's Henry VI and Richard III*; Cambridge, 1929.

HART, A. *Shakespeare and the Homilies*; Melbourne, 1934.

D'ENTRÈVES, A. P. *The medieval contribution to political thought*; Oxford, 1939.

ALLEN, J. W. *A history of political thought in the sixteenth century*, 2nd ed. 1941.

HUDSON, W. S. *John Ponet (1516?-1556), advocate of limited monarchy*; Chicago, 1942.

TILLYARD, E. M. W. *The Elizabethan world picture*, 1943.

CAMPBELL, L. B. *Shakespeare's history plays: mirrors of Elizabethan policy*; San Marino, 1947.

HALLIDAY, F. E. *Shakespeare companion, 1550-1950.* 1952.

MORRIS, C. *Political thought in England: Tyndale to Hooker*, 1953.

HONIGMANN, E. A. J. 'Shakespeare's lost source-plays'. *MLR*, XLIX, 1954, 293-307.

KNIGHTS, L. C. *Poetry, politics and the English tradition*, 1954.
——'Shakespeare's politics: with some reflections on the nature of tradition', *Proceedings of the British Academy*, XLIII, 1957, 115-32.

RIBNER, I. *The English history play in the age of Shakespeare*; Princeton, 1957
—revised ed., 1965.

WRIGHT, L. B. *Middle-class culture in Elizabethan England*, 1959
—ch. ix: 'The utility of history'.

MUIR, K. 'Source problems in the histories', *ShJ*. XCVI, 1960, 47-63.

TILLYARD, E. M. W. 'A Mirror for Magistrates revisited'. [In *Essays, literary and educational*, 1962, pp. 165-82.]

GENERAL CRITICISM

MOULTON, R. G. *Shakespeare as a dramatic artist*; Oxford, 1885.

MURRY, J. MIDDLETON. *Shakespeare*, 1936.

ALEXANDER, P. *Shakespeare's life and art*, 1939.

CHAMBERS, R. W. *Man's unconquerable mind*, 1939.

TILLYARD, E. M. W. *Shakespeare's history plays*, 1944.

PALMER, J. *Political characters of Shakespeare*, 1945.

CRAIG, H. 'Shakespeare and the history play'. [In *Joseph Quincy Adams Memorial Studies*, Washington, 1948, pp. 55–64.]

DANBY, J. F. *Shakespeare's doctrine of nature: a study of King Lear*, 1949.

MUIR, E. 'The politics of King Lear'. [In *Essays in literature and society*. 1949, pp. 31–48.]

SPENCER, T. *Shakespeare and the nature of man*; 2nd ed; New York, 1949.

GODDARD, H. C. *The meaning of Shakespeare*; Chicago, 1951.

CLEMEN, W. H. 'Anticipation and foreboding in Shakespeare's early histories', *ShS*, VI, 1953, 25–35.

FLUCHÈRE, H. *Shakespeare*, 1953.

JENKINS, H. 'Shakespeare's history plays: 1900–1951', *ShS*, VI, 1953, 1–15.

TRAVERSI, D. A. 'Shakespeare, the young dramatist'. [In *The Pelican Guide to English Literature, 2, The Age of Shakespeare*, ed. Boris Ford. 1955, pp. 179–200.]

STIRLING, B. *Unity in Shakespearian tragedy*; New York, 1956
—chapter on Richard III.

KNIGHTS, L. C. *Some Shakespearian themes*, 1959.

STRIBRNY, Z. *Shakespeare's history plays*; Prague, 1959.

REESE, M. M. *The cease of majesty: a study of Shakespeare's history plays*, 1961.

ROSSITER, A. P. *Angel with horns*, 1961.

TILLYARD, E. M. W. 'Shakespeare's historical cycle: organism or compilation?' [In *Essays, literary and educational*, 1962, pp. 39–46.[

WEBBER, J. 'The renewal of the King's symbolic role: from Richard II to Henry V', *TSLL*, IV, 1963, 530–8.

BULLOUGH, G. 'The uses of history'. [In *Shakespeare's world*, ed. J. Sutherland and J. Hurstfield, 1964, pp. 96–115.]

SPRAGUE, A. C. *Shakespeare's histories: plays for the stage*, 1964.

SEN GUPTA, S. *Shakespeare's historical plays*, 1964.

TURNER, R. Y. 'Characterization in Shakespeare's early history plays', *ELH*, XXXI, 1964, 241–58.

WAITH, E. M. (ed.), *Shakespeare, the histories: a collection of critical essays*; New York, 1965.

DEAN, L. F. 'From Richard II to Henry V: a closer view'. [In *Shakespeare: modern essays in criticism*, 2nd ed. 1967, pp. 188–205.]

BERMAN, R. 'Anarchy and order in Richard III and King John', *ShS*, XX, 1967, 51-9.

HAPGOOD, R. 'Shakespeare's thematic modes of speech: Richard II to Henry V', *ShS*, XX, 1967, 41-9.

MUIR, K. 'Image and symbol in Shakespeare's histories', *Bulletin of John Rylands Library*, L, 1967, 103-23.

RABKIN, N. *Shakespeare and the Common Understanding*, 1967.

RICHMOND, H. M. *Shakespeare's political plays*; New York, 1967.

SIBLY, J. 'The duty of revenge in Tudor and Stuart drama', *REL*, VIII, 1967, 46-54.

BROOKE, N. *Shakespeare's early tragedies*, 1968.

BURCKHARDT, S. *Shakespearean meanings*; New Jersey, 1968.

HUMPHREYS, A. R. 'Shakespeare's histories and the "emotion of multitude"', *Proceedings of the British Academy*, LIV, 1968, 265-87.

SANDERS, W. *The dramatist and the received idea*, 1968.

TRAVERSI, D. *An approach to Shakespeare, I: Henry VI to Twelfth Night*, 3rd ed, 1968.

WINNY, J. *The player king: a theme of Shakespeare's histories*, 1968.

WEISS, T. *The breath of clowns and kings: Shakespeare's early comedies and histories*, 1971.

RICHARD III

First editions: (i) The Tragedy of King Richard the third . . . 1597. [First Quarto. Facsimile, ed. W. W. Greg (1959)]; (ii) five further Quartos, 1598-1622; (iii) in the First Folio, 1623. Parallel texts of the First Quarto and First Folio with variants of the early Quartos, ed. K. Smith, Oslo, 1969.

Modern editions: Arden, ed. A. H. Thompson, 1907; New Variorum, ed. H. H. Furness, jr., Philadelphia, 1908; Yale, ed. J. R. Crawford, 1927; New Temple, ed. M. R. Ridley, 1935; Penguin, ed. G. B. Harrison, 1953; New Cambridge, ed. J. Dover Wilson, 1954; Pelican, ed. G. B. Evans, Baltimore, 1959; New Penguin, ed. E. A. J. Honigmann, 1968.

TEXTUAL STUDIES AND SOURCES

PATRICK, D. L. *The textual history of Richard III*, 1936.

GRIFFIN, W. J. 'An omission in the Folio text of Richard III', *RES*, XIII, 1937, 329-32.

WILSON, J. DOVER. 'Shakespeare's Richard III and the True Tragedy of Richard the Third, 1594', *ShQ*, III, 1952, 299–306.

WALTON, J. K. *The copy for the Folio text of Richard III*; Auckland, 1955 —reviewed by F. Bowers in *ShQ*, X, 1959, 91-6.

CAIRNCROSS, A. S. 'The Quartos and the Folio text of Richard III', *RES*, VIII, 1957, 225–33.

GEREVINI, F. S. *Il testo del Riccardo III*; Pavia, 1957.

WALTON, J. K. 'The Quarto copy for the Folio Richard III', *RES*, X, 1959, 127–40.

BOWERS, F. 'The copy for the Folio Richard III', *ShQ*, X, 1959, 541–4.

SMIDT, K. *Iniurious imposters and Richard III*; Oslo, 1964.

HINMAN, C. 'Shakespeare's text—then, now and tomorrow', *ShS*, XVIII, 1965, 23-33.

HONIGMANN, E. A. J. 'The text of Richard III', *Theatre Research*, VII, 1965, 48-55.

CRITICAL STUDIES

ALEXANDER, P. *Shakespeare's Henry VI and Richard III*, 1929.

ROSSITER, A. P. 'The structure of Richard the Third', *Durham University Journal*, XXXI, 1938, 44–75.

THOMAS, S. *The antic Hamlet and Richard III*; New York, 1943.

LAW, R. A. 'Richard III: a study in Shakespeare's composition'; *PMLA*, LX, 1945, 689–96.

SMITH, F. M. 'The relation of Macbeth to Richard III'; *PMLA*, LX, 1945, 1003–20.

CLEMEN, W. H. 'Tradition and originality in Shakespeare's Richard III', *ShQ*, V, 1954, 247–57.

——*Kommentar zu Shakespeare's Richard III: Interpretation eines Dramas*; Göttingen, 1957

—English translation by J. Bonheim, 1968.

DRIVER, T. F. *The sense of history in Greek and Shakespearean drama*; New York, 1960.

WILKES, G. A. 'An early allusion to Richard III, and its bearing on the date of the play', *ShQ*, XII, 1961, 464-5.

ANDERSON, R. L. 'The pattern of behaviour culminating in Macbeth', *SEL*, III, 1963, 151-73.

CARNALL, G. 'Shakespeare's Richard III and St Paul', *ShQ*, XIV, 1963. 186-8.

HEILMAN, R. B. 'Satiety and conscience: aspects of Richard III', *Antioch Review*, XXIV, 1964, 57-73.

MOMOSE, I. 'The temporal awareness in Richard III', *Shakespeare Studies* (Japan), III, 1964, 42-72.

BROOKE, N. 'Reflecting gems and dead bones: tragedy versus history in Richard III'. *Critical Quarterly*, VII, 1965, 123-34.

HAEFFNER, P. *A critical commentary on Shakespeare's Richard III*, 1966.

KRIEGER, M. 'The dark generations of Richard III'. [In *The play and place of criticism*; Baltimore, 1967. pp. 37-52.]

FRENCH, A. L. 'The world of Richard III' *ShSt*, IV, 1968, 25-39.

SMITH, I. 'Dramatic time versus clock time in Shakespeare', *ShQ*, XX, 1969, 65-9.

KING JOHN

First edition: in the First Folio, 1623.

Modern editions: New Variorum, ed. H. H. Furness, jr., Philadelphia, 1919; Yale, ed. S. T. Williams, 1927; New Temple, ed. M. R. Ridley, 1935; New Cambridge, ed. J. Dover Wilson, 1936; Arden, ed. E. A. J. Honigmann, 1954, revised 1967; Penguin, ed. G. B. Harrison, 1957; Pelican, ed. I. Ribner, 1962.

TEXTUAL STUDIES AND SOURCES

ELSON, J. 'Studies in the King John plays'. [In *Joseph Quincy Adams Memorial Studies*; Washington, 1948, pp. 183-97].

LAW, R. A. 'On the date of King John', *SP*, LIV, 1957, 119-27.

MCDIARMID, M. P. 'Concerning the Troublesome Reign of King John', *Notes and Queries*, CCII, 1957, 435-8.

ELLIOTT, J. R. 'Shakespeare and the double image of King John', *ShSt*, I, 1965, 64-84.

CRITICAL STUDIES

ASH, D. F. 'Anglo-French relations in King John', *Études anglaises*, III, 1939, 349-58.

PETIT-DUTAILLIS, C. *Le roi Jean et Shakespeare*; Paris, 1944.

CALDERWOOD, J. L. 'Commodity and honor in King John', *UTQ*, XXIX, 1960, 341-56.

SALTER, F. M. 'Problem of King John', *Royal Society of Canada Transactions*, XLIII, 1949, 115-36.

BONJOUR, A. 'The road to Swinstead Abbey: a study of the sense and structure of King John', *ELH*, XVIII, 1951, 253-74.

PETTET, E. C. 'Hot irons and fever: a note on some of the imagery of King John', *EC*, IV, 1954, 128-44.

VAN DE WATER, J. C. 'The Bastard in King John', *ShQ*, XI, 1960, 137-46.

STEVICK, R. D. 'Repentant ashes: the matrix of "Shakespearian" poetic language', *ShQ*, XIII, 1962, 366-70.

MATCHETT, W. H. 'Richard's divided heritage in King John', *EC*, XII, 1962, 231-53.

BONJOUR, A. 'Bastinado for the Bastard'. [In *English studies presented to R. W. Zandvoort. (English Studies* XLV); Amsterdam, 1964, pp. 169-76].

BURCKHARDT, S. 'King John: the ordering of this present time', *ELH*, XXXIII, 1966, 133-53.

SIBLY, J. 'The anomalous case of King John', *ELH*, XXXIII, 1966, 415-21.

BOKLUND, G. 'The troublesome ending of King John', *Studia Neophilologica*, XL, 1968, 175-84.

PRICE, J. R. 'King John and problematic art', *ShQ*, XXI, 1970, 25-8.

RICHARD II

First editions: (i) The Tragedie of King Richard the second . . . 1597. [First Quarto. Facsimile ed. W. A. Harrison (1888)]; (ii) four further Quartos, 1598–1615; (iii) in the First Folio, 1623.

Modern editions: New Temple, ed. M. R. Ridley, 1935; Penguin, ed. G. B. Harrison, 1937; New Clarendon, ed. J. M. Lothian, 1938; New Cambridge, ed. J. Dover Wilson, 1939; ed. G. J. Kittredge, New York, 1941; Arden, ed. P. Ure, 5th ed. 1961; New Variorum, ed. M. W. Black, Philadelphia, 1956; Yale, ed. R. T. Petersson, 1957; Pelican, ed. M. Black, Baltimore, 1957; New Penguin, ed. S. Wells, 1969.

TEXTUAL STUDIES AND SOURCES

BLACK, M. W. 'The sources of Shakespeare's Richard II'. [In *Joseph Quincy Adams Memorial Studies*. Washington, 1948, pp. 199-216.]

HASKER, R. E. 'The copy of the First Folio Richard II', *SB*, V, 1953, 53-72.

CRITICAL STUDIES

DRAPER, J. W. 'The character of Richard II', *PQ*, XXI, 1942, 228–36.

ALTICK, R. D. 'Symphonic imagery in Richard II', *PMLA*, LXII, 1947, 339–65.

RIBNER, I. 'Bolingbroke, a true Machievellian', *MLQ*, IX, 1948, 177–84.

BONNARD, G. A. 'The actor in Richard II', *ShJ*, LXXXVII–VIII, 1952, 87–101.

SUZMAN, A. 'Imagery and symbolism in Richard II'. *ShQ.*, VII, 1956, 355–70.

BRYANT, J. A. jnr. 'The linked analogies of Richard II', *Sewanee Review*, LXV, 1957, 420–33.

KANTOROWICZ, E. *The King's two bodies: a study in mediaeval political theology*; Princeton, 1957.

THOMPSON, K. F. 'Richard II, martyr', *ShQ*, VIII, 1957, 159–66.

QUINN, M. 'The King is not himself: the personal tragedy of Richard II', *SP*, LVI, 1959, 169–86.

DORIUS, R. J. 'A little more than a little', *ShQ*, XI, 1960, 13–26.

HENINGER, S. K. jr. 'The sun-king analogy in Richard II', *ShQ*, XI, 1960, 319–27.

HILL, R. F. 'Dramatic techniques and interpretation in Richard II'. [In *Early Shakespeare*, ed. J. R. Brown and B. Russell, 1961, pp. 101–21.]

HUTCHISON, H. F. 'Shakespeare and Richard II', *History Today*, XI, 1961, 236–44.

PHIALAS, P. G. 'The medieval in Richard II', *ShQ*, XII, 1961, 305–10.

ANDERSON, D. K. jr. 'Richard II and Perkin Warbeck', *ShQ*, XIII, 1962, 260–3.

PROVOST, G. F. 'The sorrows of Shakespeare's Richard II'. [In *Studies in English Renaissance Literature*, ed. W. F. McNeir; Baton Rouge, 1962, pp. 40–55.]

TALBERT, E. W. *The problem of world order*, 1962.

BROOKS, H. F. 'Shakespeare and the Governour, Bk II, ch. xiii; parallels with Richard II and the "More" addition', *ShQ*, XIV, 1963, 195–9.

HAPGOOD, R. 'Three eras in Richard II', *ShQ*, XIV, 1963, 281–3.

PHIALAS, P. G. 'Richard II and Shakespeare's tragic mode', *TSLL*, V, 1963, 344–55.

HALSTEAD, W. L. 'Artifice and artistry in Richard II and Othello'. [In *Sweet smoke of rhetoric*, ed. N. G. Lawrence and J. A. Reynolds; Coral Gables, 1964, pp. 19–51.]

HOCKEY, D. C. 'A world of rhetoric in Richard II', *ShQ*, XV, 1964, 179-91.

REIMAN, D. H. 'Appearance, reality and moral order in Richard II', *MLQ*, XXV, 1964, 34-45.

ELLIOTT, J. R. 'Richard II and the medieval', *Renaissance Papers*, 1965, 25-34.

HUMPHREYS, A. 'Shakespeare's political justice in Richard II and Henry IV', *Stratford Papers on Shakespeare*, V, 1965, 30-50.

SPEAIGHT, R. 'Shakespeare and the political spectrum: as illustrated by Richard II', *Stratford Papers on Shakespeare*, V, 1965, 135-54.

TRAVERSI, D. 'Richard II', *Stratford Papers on Shakespeare*, V, 1965, 11-29.

FRENCH, A. L. 'Who deposed Richard the Second?', *EC*, XVII, 1967, 411-33.

HUMPHREYS, A. R. *Shakespeare's Richard II*, 1967.

ELLIOTT, J. R. 'History and tragedy in Richard II', *SEL*, VIII, 1968, 253-71.

FRENCH, A. L. 'Richard II: a rejoinder', *EC*, XVIII, 1968, 229-33.

URE, P. 'Richard II, or "To find out right with wrong" ', *EC*, XVIII, 1968, 225-9.

JEFFARES, A. N. 'In one person many peoples: King Richard the Second'. [In *The morality of art; essays presented to G. Wilson Knight*, ed. D. W. Jefferson; New York, 1969.]

WICKHAM, G. *Shakespeare's dramatic heritage*, 1969.

GRIVELET, M. 'Shakespeare's "war with time": the sonnets and Richard II', *ShS*, XXIII, 1970, 69-78.

HARTSOCK, M. E. 'Major scenes in minor key', *ShQ*, XXI, 1970, 55-62.

HENRY V

First editions: (i) The Chronicle History of Henry the fifth . . . 1600. [A 'bad' Quarto. Facsimile ed. W. W. Greg (1957)]; (ii) in the First Folio, 1623.

Modern editions: New Temple, ed. M. R. Ridley, 1935; Penguin, ed. G. B. Harrison, 1937; New Clarendon, ed. R. F. W. Fletcher, 1941; ed. G. L. Kittredge, New York, 1945; New Cambridge, ed. J. Dover Wilson, 1947; Arden, ed. J. H. Walter, 1954; Yale, ed. R. J. Dorius, 1955; Pelican, ed. L. B. Wright and V. Freund, Baltimore, 1957; New Penguin, ed. A. R. Humphreys, 1968.

TEXTUAL STUDIES AND SOURCES

SMITH, W. D. 'The Henry V choruses in the First Folio', *JEGP*, LIII, 1954, 38–57.

CAIRNCROSS, A. S. 'Quarto copy for Folio Henry V', *SB*, VIII, 1956, 67–93.

WALKER, A. 'Some editorial principles, with special reference to Henry V', *SB*, VIII, 1956, 95–112.

PITCHER, S. M. *The case for Shakespeare's authorship of The Famous Victories*; New York, 1961.

DUTHIE, G. L. 'The Quarto of Shakespeare's Henry V'. [In *Papers mainly Shakespearian*; Edinburgh, 1964.]

CRITICAL STUDIES

TRAVERSI, D. A. 'Henry the Fifth', *Scrutiny*, IX, 1941, 352–74.

WILSON, J. DOVER. *The fortunes of Falstaff*; Cambridge, 1943.

JORGENSEN, P. A. 'Accidental judgments, casual slaughters and purposes mistook: critical reactions to Shakespere's Henry V', *Shakespeare Association Bulletin*, XXII, 1947, 51–61.

——'The courtship scene in Henry V', *MLQ*, XI, 1950, 180–8.

RIBNER, I. 'The political problem in Shakespeare's Lancastrian tetralogy', *SP*, XLIX, 1952, 171–84.

BRADDY, H. 'Shakespeare's Henry V and the French nobility', *TSLL*, III, 1961, 189–96.

DICKINSON, H. 'Reformation of Prince Hal', *ShQ*, XII, 1961, 33–46.

FLEISSNER, R. F. 'Falstaff's green sickness unto death', *ShQ*, XII, 1961, 47–55.

PRICE, G. R. 'Henry V and Germanicus', *ShQ*, XII, 1961, 57–60.

BATTENHOUSE, R. W. 'Henry V as heroic comedy'. [In *Essays on Shakespeare and Elizabethan drama in honor of Hardin Craig*, ed. R. Hosley; Columbia, Mo., 1962, pp. 163–82.]

STRIBRNY, Z. 'Henry V and history'. [*Shakespeare in a changing world: essays*, ed. A. Kettle, 1964, pp. 84–101.]

BARISH, J. A. 'The turning away of Prince Hal'. *SStud*, I, 1965, 9–17.

PHIALAS, P. G. 'Shakespeare's Henry V and the second tetralogy'. *SP*, LXII, 1965, 155–75.

BASU, K. 'Julius Caesar and Henry V'. [In *Shakespeare Commemoration Volume*, ed. Taraknath Sen; Calcutta, 1966, pp. 89–124.]

SCOUFOS, A. L. 'The martyrdom of Falstaff'. *ShSt*, II, 1966, 174–91.

HUTCHISON, H. F. 'Shakespeare and Henry V', *History Today*, XVIII, 1967, 510-17.

O'BRIEN, M. A. *A Critical commentary on Shakespeare's Henry V*, 1967.

BERMAN, R. (ed.). *Twentieth century interpretations of Henry V*; Englewood Cliffs, 1968.

BETTS, J. H. 'Classical allusions in Shakespeare's Henry V with special reference to Virgil', *Greece and Rome*, XV, 1968, 147-63.

EGAN, R. 'A Muse of fire: Henry V in the light of Tamburlaine', *MLQ*, XXIX, 1968, 15-28.

HOBDAY, C. H. 'Imagery and irony in Henry V', *ShS*, XXI, 1968, 107-14.

BARBER, C. 'Prince Hal, Henry V and the Tudor monarchy'. [In *The morality of art: essays presented to G. Wilson Knight*, ed. D. W. Jefferson; New York, 1969, pp. 67-75.]

JAMESON, T. H. *The Hidden Shakespeare*; New York, 1969.

KELLY, R. L. 'Shakespeare's Scroops and the "Spirit of Cain" ', *ShQ*, XX, 1969, 71-80.

QUINN, M. *Shakespeare: Henry V, a casebook*, 1969.

SJOBERG, E. 'From madcap prince to King: the evolution of Prince Hal', *ShQ*, XX, 1969, 11-16.

WILLIAMSON, M. L. 'The episode with Williams in Henry V', *SEL*, IX, 1969, 275-82.

THE WORKS OF WILLIAM SHAKESPEARE

GRAMOPHONE RECORDS

Under the auspices of the British Council, the complete works of Shakespeare have been recorded in stereo, in the text of the New Shakespeare edited by John Dover Wilson, with the Marlowe Society of Cambridge University and leading professional players, directed by George Rylands, Fellow of King's College; Musical director Thurston Dart. Among professional players who took part were:

MAX ADRIAN	IAN MCKELLEN
PEGGY ASHCROFT	MARY MORRIS
JILL BALCON	ANN MORRISH
MICHAEL BATES	PETER PEARS
ANNA CALDER-MARSHALL	MARGARET RAWLINGS
TONY CHURCH	CORIN REDGRAVE
WILLIAM DEVLIN	DIANA RIGG
ROY DOTRICE	PRUNELLA SCALES
ROBERT EDDISON	MARGARETTA SCOTT
JOHN GIELGUD	WILLIAM SQUIRE
DEREK GODFREY	JOHN STRIDE
IAN HOLM	JANET SUZMAN
MICHAEL HORDERN	DOROTHY TUTIN
RICHARD JOHNSON	GARY WATSON
BEATRIX LEHMANN	IRENE WORTH
MILES MALLESON	RICHARD WORDSWORTH
GERALDINE MCEWAN	PATRICK WYMARK

The productions are recorded in monaural and stereophonic sound and issued by the Argo Record Co. Ltd., 113 Fulham Road, London, SW3. The following are available:

ALL'S WELL THAT ENDS WELL	ZPR	229–31	HENRY IV Part 1	ZPR	149–52
			HENRY IV Part 2	ZPR	153–6
ANTONY AND CLEOPATRA	ZPR	221–4	HENRY V	ZPR	157–60
			HENRY VI Part 1	ZPR	161–3
AS YOU LIKE IT	ZPR	180–2	HENRY VI Part 2	ZPR	164–7
THE COMEDY OF ERRORS	ZPR	124–5	HENRY VI Part 3	ZPR	168–71
			HENRY VIII	ZPR	176–9
CORIOLANUS	ZPR	225–8	JULIUS CAESAR	ZPR	218–20
CYMBELINE	ZPR	240–3	KING JOHN	ZPR	142–5
HAMLET	ZPR	192–6	KING LEAR	ZPR	197–200

WRITERS AND THEIR WORK